A Portrait of Stoke City F.C.

in the 60s & 70s

Formed by ex-pupils of the Charterhouse School whilst working for the North Staffordshire railway, Stoke City are one of the oldest football teams in the world.

The first recorded match played by the team known as the Stoke Ramblers took place in 1868 when they managed a 1-1 draw against another team of railway workers, the EW May XV.

The club merged with Stoke Victoria Cricket Club in March 1878 and switched from Sweetings Field to the Athletic Club ground. The site became known as the Victoria Ground and was the club's home for the next 119 years.

As long and eventful as the club's history is, the most thrilling and unquestionably glamorous period for Stoke City came in the 1960s and 70s. The decade started off badly. Dwindling crowds and poor performances on the pitch meant that prospects for Stoke City were grim.

Quality young players were being churned out of Stoke's famous youth systems' but unfortunately the manager Frank Taylor could not do enough to pull the club around and his assistant Tony Waddington took control of the team in June 1960.

Waddington presided over a defence that had conceded 83 goals during the previous campaign and he quickly realised that new tactics were needed in order to make the team harder to beat.

"Waddington's Wall" was the term that became associated with Stoke's newfound defensive stability and, although

Stoke only retained their Second Division status by three points during the new manager's first season, the general consensus was that the corner had now been turned.

Attendances were still disturbingly low, averaging slightly fewer than 9,000, and Waddington knew that this problem would have to be dealt with. He pulled off an absolute masterstroke by enticing the already legendary Stanley Matthews back to the club in 1961.

A huge crowd of 35,974 crammed into the Victoria Ground to witness the return of their hero to the club where his epic achievements had begun. He was 46 years old at the time but his class and influence shone through, causing a surge in form that led to the team finishing in eighth place and looking forward with much optimism to the 1962/63 centenary season.

That confidence proved to be well founded as Stoke City took the league by storm, securing promotion and winning the Second Division title as Matthews worked his magic on the wing. Stoke proudly took their place in the top echelon of English football and their stay proved to be a long and fruitful one.

Waddington knew experience was what his team needed in order to remain in the top flight and he began to bring in players others regarded as being past their best. Jackie Mudie, Dennis Viollet, Maurice Setters, Roy Vernon and Jimmy McIlroy all became members of a Stoke City team who began to build a reputation for exciting and effective football.

The team even had a knight in their ranks after Stanley Matthews was rewarded for his services to football in the 1965 New Year's honours list. Soon after, Sir Stanley Matthews played his 701st and final league game, against Fulham, at the age of 50.

The impact of losing such an important player was lessened when Waddington pulled off another great signing, luring Gordon Banks, at that time arguably the world's best goalkeeper, to the club for a fee of £52,000.

Although Stoke City were a club renowned all over the world, they had never managed to land a major trophy. This was to change in 1972 when they captured the League Cup with a thrilling victory over Chelsea in front of a huge 97,852 Wembley crowd.

Waddington had built a great team that really should have captured more than just the one major trophy. In fact, they lost to Arsenal in successive F.A Cup semi-finals and became one of the most feared cup teams around at the time.

Great home grown players such as Alan Bloor, Eric Skeels, John Marsh, Denis Smith and Mike Pejic became mainstays during the 1970s and strikers such as John Ritchie and Jimmy Greenhoff struck fear into the hearts of many a team. Sadly however, Gordon Banks was forced to retire after losing an eye in a road accident in October 1972.

Waddington knew that his team were ageing and that new blood had to be brought in to replace those players whose better days were behind them. The signing of Alan Hudson from Chelsea in 1974

proved to be a huge success. His vision and skill in the centre of the park sent Stoke City on a run that nearly secured them the league title.

The decade also saw the club's only ventures into European competition. They were defeated by Kaiserslauten of Germany in the 1972/73 UEFA Cup and two years later Ajax knocked them out of the same competition after two extremely tight games.

Unfortunately, the last few years of the 1970s were not kind to the club. A storm destroyed part of the Butler Street Stand in January 1976 and the cost of fixing the damage precipitated financial problems that led to the club having to sell some of their best players.

The loss of Hudson, Pejic and Greenhoff altered the club immensely and Stoke were relegated at the end of the 1976/77 season, prompting the departure of Tony Waddington after 17 productive years in charge. George Eastham, who could do nothing to reverse the declining fortunes of the club, replaced him, but only stayed with the club for a short time.

Results picked up after Alan Durban became the new manager with Howard Kendall coming in as player/coach. This duo introduced new ideas and promotion back into the First Division was secured on the final day of the 1978/79 season.

The eighties were a bad time for football as a whole. Hooliganism was on the rise and attendances steadily declined. The period also signalled the departure of many of Stoke's most loved players. The remaining members of the great 1970s teams such as Denis Smith, Jackie Marsh and Terry Conroy left the club and although exciting young stars like Garth Crooks and Lee Chapman replaced them, the fortunes of Stoke City F.C. suffered the blow of relegation in 1984/85.

Since then it has been very much a roller coaster of emotion for Stoke City fans. Promotions, relegations, changes of management and ownership of the club have all been witnessed. The 1995/96 season was probably Stoke's best chance of reaching the promised land of the Premiership. Lou Macari so nearly led the club to promotion, but was stopped by Leicester in the semi-finals of the play-offs.

Stoke relocated from the Victoria Ground to the 28,000 seater Britannia Stadium after the 1996/97 season, it should have heralded a change in fortunes and a place in the top echelons of British football. Contained in the following chapters are a range of photographs and information, which reveal the amazing history of Stoke City F.C. The passion and loyalty that fans have shown the club throughout its long existance can be seen time and time again inside this book.

Contents

When Tony Waddington took over from Frank Taylor as manager of the Potters in June 1960, he faced quite a challenge. The club had been steadily producing promising youngsters but had not witnessed success on the pitch for quite some time.

Waddington knew that things had to change. He brought a new defensive stability to the team as well as a group of hugely experienced players that helped turn things around for Stoke City.

Without doubt his most famous signing during this period was Stanley Matthews. Already a Potteries legend, the return of Matthews to the club in 1961 led to a huge upturn in attendances at the Victoria Ground.

Although 47 years old, Matthews played an important role in the promotion that the club clinched during its centenary year in 1962. He was eventually honoured for his services to the sport and became Sir Stanley Matthews at the beginning of 1965.

Only defeat to Leicester City in the 1964 League Cup final put a dampener on affairs at the Victoria Ground. Stoke had easily secured promotion and Waddington proved himself to be absolutely invaluable.

Stoke City skipper Bobby Howitt congratulates Stanley Matthews after his return "debut" for the club in 1961. The opponents on that day were Huddersfield Town and a huge crowd of 35,974 filled the Victoria Ground in order to witness the return of their hero.

Stoke City players are pictured here during a training session on a typically blustery autumn day. Amongst them (from left to right) are Don Ratcliffe, Jackie Mudie, Graham Matthews and Tony Allen.

Jackie Mudie gets a pass to Thompson through the legs of Jones, the Middlesbrough left-back.
The game, played at the Victoria Ground, finished with a 2-0 Stoke victory. As well as Sir Stan and
Mudie, other experienced players were enticed to the club by the astute management of Waddington in
the 1960s. Players such as Dennis Viollet, Roy Vernon, Maurice Setters and Jimmy McIlroy also became
Stoke City regulars. Mudie joined the club for £7,000 from Blackpool in March 1961. He had been
capped 17 times for Scotland and was in the Blackpool team that won the F.A Cup final against Bolton in
1953. Mudie was 30 years old and went on to score 33 goals in 93 appearances for the Potters.

Tony Waddington was widely regarded as the best manager that Stoke City ever had. In his long and successful tenure at the club he won the League Cup, as well as challenging for many other honours, including the FA Cup and the First Division Championship, on a number of occasions.

Stoke City in 1963. Pictured on the back row (from left to right) are Allen, Clamp, Asprey, O'Neill, Stuart and Skeels. On the front row are: Matthews, Vincent, Mudie, McIlroy and Ratcliffe.

Members of the Stoke City squad take a well-deserved break from football as they enjoy a pleasant afternoon at the swimming pool.

John Farmer in athletic form during a training session in the early 1960s. Farmer came through the ranks at Stoke City and spent 10 years with the club, making 163 appearances and playing a vital role as an understudy to Gordon Banks. He left Stoke to join Northwich Victoria.

Some of Stoke City's young players are put through their paces during training. The once familiar factories, mills and potbanks seen in the background gradually disappeared as the pottery industry declined.

As an experienced member of the Stoke City team, Tony Allen was the ideal person to help out the younger players. After starting out in the junior team, Allen went on to play 417 league games for the Potters.

Before signing for Stoke City, Peter Dobing had represented great teams such as Manchester City and Blackburn Rovers. Dobing spent the rest of his illustrious career with the Potters, finally having his playing days cut short in 1973 after he broke his leg in a match against Ipswich Town in 1972.

Bill Bentley practises his skills during a training session for Stoke City. He made 48 appearances for the club before being transferred to Blackpool in 1969.

Graham Matthews played as a forward in the Stoke City youth teams before graduating to the seniors. He only played 16 league games, scoring 5 goals, before being sold to Walsall in 1963.

Stoke City schoolboys (from left to right) Michael Broad, Bill Bentley and John Marsh. Michael Broad failed to appear for the club in any first team matches. Bill Bentley played for the club between 1965-69 and made 48 appearances. John Marsh was at the club between 1967-79 making an impressive 355 league appearances before going to Northwich Victoria.

Congratulations were the order of the day as Stoke City's jubilant fans saw their heroes presented with yet another trophy.

Stoke City fans had an extremely enjoyable day out on the 4 January 1964 when they defeated Portsmouth 4-1 in the third round of the F.A Cup.

Alan Philpott and Peter Dobing keeping the ball up in the air during a training session. Philpott played for Stoke City between 1960-68 and made 45 league appearances, before being sold to Oldham Athletic.

When the football is over there is still much to do. Workmen are pictured here rigging up the floodlights for the Victoria Ground that granted such special atmosphere to evening matches.

Jimmy McIlroy is seen here showing the supreme effort that epitomised his tenure with the club. After signing from Burnley in 1963, McIlroy went on to make 98 league appearances and scored many goals before joining Oldham Athletic as player/manager.

Stoke winger Harry Burrows attempts to score with a long-range shot. Burrows appeared 245 times in the league for Stoke City and scored 68 goals between 1965-73 before leaving the club for Plymouth Argyle.

A smiling Stanley Matthews pictured during training for Stoke City in 1964. Sitting with him are Tony Allen and goalkeeper Jimmy O'Neill. O'Neill joined the club from Everton in 1960 and played 130 league games for Stoke City before moving to Darlington.

Attendances at the Victoria Ground had been restored to healthy numbers due mainly to the return of Stanley Matthews to the club. A packed house is seen admiring the skills of the "Wizard of Dribble".

The club celebrated its centenary in 1963 by organising a friendly match against the most glamorous European club of all time. A crowd of nearly 45,000 turned up to witness Stoke City face Real Madrid. The match was a huge success and lucky fans were able to see such legendary names as Alfredo Di Stefano and Ferenc Puskas. Below the Spanish team are captured as they train at the Victoria Ground.

The great Sir Stanley Matthews seen here leaving the tunnel and leading his men out on to the pitch against the world famous Real Madrid team in 1963. Fans flocked to the Victoria Ground to witness this amazing clash, which ended in a 2-2 draw.

A crowd of nearly 45,000 turned up to witness Stoke City face Real Madrid. The match was a huge success and the Spanish players said they had never received such a warm welcome as the one given to them by Stoke City fans.

Gaskell, the Manchester United reserve goalkeeper punches out a shot from the wing, beating Stoke City reserve centre-forward John Woodward to the ball. Woodward only played 11 times for the first team before being sold to Aston Villa in 1966.

John Ritchie captured battling with the Fulham defence at Craven Cottage during the 1964/65 season. Stoke obtained a great 4-1 away win in this game.

Attendances during the early 1960s fell drastically. A ghostly Victoria Ground is seen here. Empty seats seemingly out number those in which lone fans are seated.

White Hart Lane was the venue for this exciting 2-2 draw between Tottenham Hotspur and Stoke City. Pictured here is the first Spurs goal flying into the Stoke City net.

Stoke obtained a good result in this game, beating Blackburn Rovers 3-1. 1964 proved to be a good year for Stoke City as they progressed to their first major final in the League Cup. Unfortunately they lost to Leicester 3-2 over two legs.

Stoke City players are seen here training for their cup-tie against Manchester United at the Victoria Ground. Left to right are Gerry Bridgewood, Lawrie Leslie, Bill Asprey, George Kinnell, Bobby Irvine and Kevin Palmer. The first leg was drawn 0-0 but Manchester United defeated Stoke 1-0 at Old Trafford. In a amazing turn of events Stoke City played the Manchester club three times in the space of 10 days during 1965.

Brian Sherratt was a goalkeeper for the senior team at the club between 1961-62. However, he only made a single appearance before moving to Oxford United in 1962.

Chapter 2
1965-70

Stoke City had a couple of scrapes with relegation during this period but the manager and the players always kept their place in the top echelons of the game.

Waddington made another great signing when he secured Gordon Banks from Leicester for £52,000 in 1967. Banks was widely regarded as one of the best goalkeepers in the world.

The rest of the 60s was a steady and increasingly exciting period for the club. No major honours were obtained but Stoke consolidated their place in Division One and had many memorable matches against other giants of the game such as Manchester United, Liverpool, West Ham and Arsenal.

Great players such as Dennis Viollet and Jackie Mudie added their considerable skills to a young team featuring local players such as Alan Bloor and Denis Smith and Stoke began to forge a reputation for the exciting football that was to see them challenging for honours just a few years later.

Peter Dobing is seen here spending some well-earned time away from football. The Stoke legend, who made 307 league appearances for the club between 1963-73, was also a keen angler, as well as an extremely capable cricketer.

Dobing scores the first goal for Stoke City during their 1967 game against Chelsea at Stamford Bridge past a helpless Peter Bonetti. This game ended in a 2-2 draw, but Stoke went on to overcome Chelsea in the most important game of their club history in the League Cup Final in 1972.

Dennis Viollet (left) pictured before his last game for Stoke City against Leicester City. Sitting next to him is Gordon Banks who was making his Stoke debut. The two legends crossed paths very briefly in 1967. After 182 league games and numerous goals, Viollet moved on to play for Baltimore Boys in the U.S.A.

Stoke City players Eric Skeels, Mike Bernard and Gordon Banks were amongst those players who reported for pre-season training. Skeels had a long and successful career for Stoke City, making a hugely impressive 507 league appearances between 1960-76 before leaving the club for local rivals Port Vale.

Stoke City goalkeeper Gordon Banks in typically acrobatic form, leaps to block a shot from Arsenal inside-left Sammels in the opening First Division match of the soccer season at Highbury on the 19 August 1967.

Banks manages to get the ball out of play as a relieved Jackie Marsh looks on. Marsh was a product of the Stoke City youth system. A fine overlapping full-back, he went on to appear in 433 league and cup games before leaving the club to join Northwich Victoria in 1979.

John Ritchie challenges the Tottenham Hotspur goalkeeper during
the 1967/68 season. Stoke managed a 2-1 victory in this game.

The spirit amongst teammates at Stoke City was always one of the main reasons for the club's success. Amongst those seen here are David Herd, Gordon Banks and George Eastham.

Gordon Banks dives despairingly but can do nothing to prevent Peter Osgood's drive flying past him into the net during the 2-2 draw with Chelsea in September 1967. Banks may have let two goals past him on this occasion but his presence throughout the decade stabilised Stoke City's defence greatly.

Stoke City footballers reporting for training at the Victoria Ground. Left to right are Gordon Banks, Peter Dobing, Maurice Setters, Terry Conroy, George Eastham and Tony Allen. The photo was taken in 1968, the year after Stoke City signed Gordon Banks.

Stoke City training at the Victoria Ground in October 1967. The club narrowly avoided relegation during this season, but better things were definitely to come over the next few years.

Banks clears the ball from the head of Everton's centre-forward Joe Royle, watched on by Stoke players Alan Bloor and Mike Pejic. Bloor's potential was spotted as a schoolboy and he went on to become an apprentice with Stoke before winning youth international caps for England. He completed 18 full seasons with the Potters racking up 474 league and cup appearances.

Jimmy McIlroy is seen here challenging West Ham's John Bond for the ball at Upton Park. Waddington signed him (McIlroy) from Burnley for £25,000. He went on to score 16 goals in 98 league appearances before becoming player/manager of Oldham Athletic.

Stoke City defender Eric Skeels heads the ball back into the safe arms of Gordon Banks. Skeels played an amazing 507 times in the league for Stoke City.

Stoke's centre-forward John Ritchie out-jumps two Everton players and heads towards goal only to see his effort saved by Andy Rankin, the Everton keeper. Ritchie was a superb striker who excelled in the air.

Everton's Joe Royle forces the ball over the line to beat Stoke's keeper Gordon Banks as full-back Mike Pejic attempts to make the challenge. Pejic was renowned as an extremely competent defender and made 274 league appearances for the club before moving on to Everton in 1977.

Joe Royle challenges Gordon Banks for the ball. An unlucky Stoke City defender is trapped in the middle.

Gordon Banks, Peter Dobing and Tony Waddington are seen in an official capacity representing Stoke City F.C in the community. Taken on the 31 July 1968.

Terry Lees, centre, the captain of Stoke's youth team pictured training with Alan Dodd, Tommy Walker, Ray Brown and Steve Mason for an up-coming F.A Youth Cup quarter-final tie at Tottenham.

This picture perfectly demonstrates the kind of weather conditions that football players in the 1960s had to endure. A slick, muddy surface did not encourage the type of football that fans love to see.

Tottenham Hotspur striker Alan Gilzean shoots past Stoke goalkeeper Gordon Banks to give Spurs their second goal in the 3-0 victory at White Hart Lane. Martin Chivers of Tottenham looks on.

Stoke City keeper John Farmer just could not hold on to Arsenal player Terry Neill's penalty shot. Neill finally put the ball into the back of the net for Arsenal's first goal in the Division One game at Highbury.

Players congratulate each other as they trudge off the pitch after the end of another tough game for Stoke City.

Crowd control at football matches was a very different proposition prior to the 1980s. Here is a peaceful scene showing a solitary policeman making sure the supporters are behaving themselves.

George Eastham (left) scored the winning goal in the 2-1 victory against Chelsea; it was his first goal for 18 months. Eastham represented Stoke from 1966-73 and played 194 times in the league before retiring from the playing side and becoming a well-respected coach at the club.

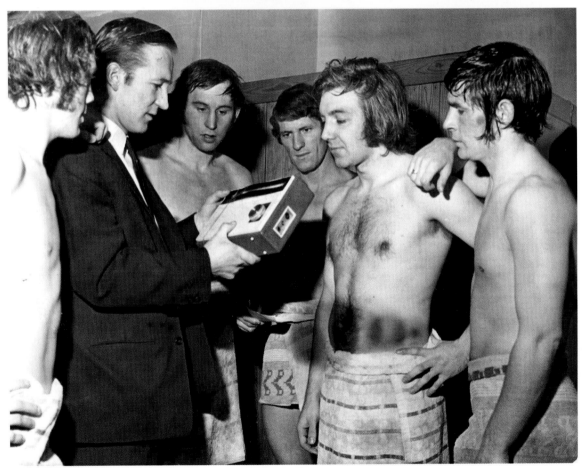

Peter Dobing, captain of Stoke City, anxiously listens for news on a cup draw as other squad players look on.

Stoke's Dennis Viollet and John Farmer head out on to the pitch at the Victoria Ground. Viollet played 182 league games and scored 59 goals during his 5-year tenure at the club.

Albert Quixall is seen here arriving at the Victoria Ground with his good friend Dennis Viollet. Viollet was an integral part of the legendary Busby Babes before joining Stoke in 1962. He remained at the club for 6 years and scored an impressive 59 goals in 182 league games. Quixall also played for Manchester United in the years following the Munich air disaster in 1958, winning an F.A Cup medal in 1963.

Frank Mountford was a hugely experienced player for Stoke City, making almost 200 wartime appearances for the club, and scoring over 50 goals. During his football career he moved from playing as a centre-forward to wing-half, then centre-half and finally to full-back. After 425 games in total for the Potters he retired as a player but stayed with the club, first as a trainer then as a coach.

Gordon Banks is seen here carrying equipment off the training ground.

An unlucky John Ritchie sees his almost perfect header saved by Everton's Andy Rankin. Ritchie was a player renowned for his prowess in the air.

John Farmer was one
of a number of Stoke
players who graduated
from Stoke's famous
youth academies and
went on to represent the
club. Players such as
Alan Bloor, Mike Pejic
and Denis Smith all
came through the ranks.

Gordon Banks demonstrates that football is not the only sport he has tried his hand at.
Looked on by his Stoke City colleagues, Banks attempts to block a cricket ball with the
same flair he showed for stopping goals.

Left: John Mahoney salutes the Stoke City fans at the Victoria Ground. Mahoney, a Welsh international, had a distinguished playing career before enjoying success as a manager.

John Ritchie celebrates after yet another goal for Stoke City. Ritchie was signed for £2,500 from Kettering on a scout's recommendation. He went on to spend two glorious spells with the club.

Manchester United's Bobby Charlton looks on as Stoke City attacker John Mahoney beats him to the ball in front of a huge Old Trafford crowd.

Seven defenders rush out to try to prevent Peter Dobing demonstrating the technique that led him to over 350 appearances at Stoke City, many of them as captain of the team.

Stoke's players are crowded and shot from every possible angle by a hoard of photographers.

Media coverage is a vital part of the game. Here a smiling player looks on as a television crew interviews one of his colleagues in the late 1960s.

Chapter 3
1970-75

After 109 years in existence, Stoke City finally managed to grab a piece of major silverware on 4 March 1972 by beating Chelsea in the final of the League Cup in front of a huge Wembley crowd. Fans of Stoke City were at last able to experience the pleasure and pride of a major victory.

The next day, the streets of Stoke-on-Trent were packed with over 250,000 ecstatic Stoke City fans. With a little more luck this kind of scene could have been repeated time and again as Waddington had moulded a highly effective team.

Homegrown talent such as Eric Skeels, John Marsh and Mike Pejic all worked extremely hard and kept up the best traditions of Stoke City on the field of play. And strikers such as John Ritchie and Jimmy Greenhoff were renowned all over Europe for both their effectiveness and aggression.

The team were knocked out of the FA Cup at the semi-final stage in two consecutive years. Arsenal proved to be the stumbling block both times as the team from Highbury twice dented Stoke City's FA Cup dreams.

Under Waddington's tenure Stoke also made a couple of serious title challenges. The manager added to his team talented individuals such as Alan Hudson and Geoff Salmons and Stoke went heart-breakingly close to capturing the First Division title only to fall away right at the end of the 1974/75 season.

Mike Bernard gives Tony Waddington a laugh by bowing in respect to him before the start of a testimonial game. Bernard played for the club between 1966-72, making 134 appearances and scoring 6 goals from midfield. He eventually left Stoke City to join Everton.

Liverpool F.C's John Toshack challenges Denis Smith during their 1-0 victory at the Victoria Ground on the 10 April 1971. Toshack had an incredible career for Liverpool and Wales before becoming a highly successful manager for many clubs including two stints at Real Madrid. Smith himself had a great managerial career with York City, Bristol City, Sunderland and Oxford.

Mike Pejic looks on as Gordon Banks dives at the feet of a Liverpool attacker in front of a packed Anfield Stadium.

Everton's goalkeeper Andy Rankin jumps in the air to clear a cross as John Ritchie and Alan Bloor look on. Also in the picture is Everton's Howard Kendall, who later went on to play and coach Stoke City.

Peter Dobing leads out Stoke City during the 1970s. Emerging from the changing rooms behind Dobing are Denis Smith and Gordon Banks, some of Stoke's most famous and well-respected players of all time.

The legendary West Ham skipper Bobby Moore is seen here in action against Stoke City at the Victoria Ground. Moore famously captained the 1966 World-Cup winning side that also contained a certain Geoff Hurst, who went on to play for the Potters.

Geoff Hurst is seen here in action for Stoke City during their encounter with Leeds United. The match took place on the 9 September 1972 ending in a 2-2 draw.

West Ham keeper Bobby Ferguson manages to pluck a high cross out of the air and away from Stoke City's Peter Dobing and Jimmy Greenhoff.

With nearly 1,000 appearances between them Willie Stevenson, Peter Dobing, Gordon Banks, Harry Burrows and Terry Conroy played a significant part in the success the club experienced in the 1970s.

John Ritchie celebrates after scoring yet another goal. Ritchie netted a hugely impressive 171 goals during his two spells with the club. In fact he remains Stoke City's record goalscorer to this day.

Some of Stoke City's youth team players are pictured here with club captain Peter Dobing. They are showing off the commemorative mugs that were manufactured to celebrate the 1972 League Cup final victory.

Gordon Banks seen here with three youngsters who took penalty kicks against the England keeper for a London T.V penalty kick competition. The lucky fans are Raymond Taylor, Kevin Palmer and Bill Jenkins.

Twins Tony and Trevor Fairbanks are in the centre of this group of young footballers who signed associate schoolboy forms with Stoke City. Left to right are Paul Bradbury, Tony and Trevor Fairbanks and Ian Miller. At the rear are Peter Hollins, Lee Chapman and Stuart Ecclestone. Unfortunately only Lee Chapman went on to have a significant career at the club. He made 99 appearances and scored 34 goals before moving to Arsenal in 1982.

Manchester City's celebrated goalkeeper Joe Corrigan tips the ball away from a Stoke forward as Mike Doyle and Glyn Pardo look on.

A perplexed Tony Book of Manchester City looks on as Jimmy Greenhoff scores yet another goal in Stoke's 5-1 demolition of the Division One club on the 23 September 1972.

Gordon Banks punches a header from Manchester United's George Best during the clash between the sides at Old Trafford.

John Ritchie is seen here in typically robust mood. Ritchie remains the most prolific goalscorer in the history of Stoke City with 171 League and Cup goals. He netted 59 times in his first 91 games before being inexplicably sold to Sheffield Wednesday in November 1966 for £70,000. Although he returned to the Potters in 1969 and remained until 1975.

Alan A'Court after a training session in 1972. A good-natured player he went on to take a large role in representing the team in public affairs.

Alan Bloor, the Stoke City defender heads the ball above a Kaiserslautern defender during Stoke's brief UEFA Cup run in 1972. Stoke made very few forays into European Competition during the 1970s. The German side knocked them out in 1972 in a 5-3 aggregate defeat and two years later Dutch team Ajax delivered the knockout blow on away goals.

Geoff Hurst demonstrates
the attributes that made
him such a feared opponent.

Peter Shilton leads out Stoke City for their Division One clash against Middlesbrough which
Stoke won 1-0.

Geoff Hurst glances through the pages of an Evening Sentinel in order to find the story of the day.

Denis Smith looks on despairingly as West Ham's Billy Bonds gets a header on target when the two teams clashed on the 17 April 1971. On the left of the picture is Geoff Hurst, the England star, still the only man to score a hat-trick in a World Cup final, signed for Stoke from West Ham in 1972 and made 108 league appearances, netting 30 goals.

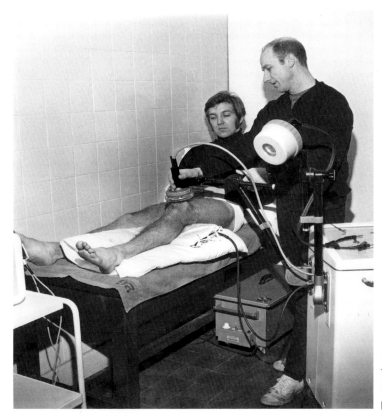

Mark Bernard receives treatment on his injured knee from a Stoke City physiotherapist.

Jimmy Greenhoff attempts to beat the Arsenal goalkeeper as Frank McLintock looks on despairingly. Greenhoff was a popular player in his time at Stoke, securing a transfer to Manchester United in 1976.

Jimmy Greenhoff, Denis Smith, Geoff Hurst and Jackie Marsh celebrate the capture of the Watney Cup in 1973. The Watney Cup was Britain's first commercially sponsored tournament and was a pre-season competition for the two top scoring teams in each division of the Football league. Stoke won the competition in 1973/74, the last time it was played. They beat Plymouth Argyle, Bristol City and Hull. Jimmy Greenhoff scored both goals in the final.

Stoke were a much-feared cup team in the 1970s. On this occasion in 1971, early round victims Southport were despatched comfortably 2-0.

Peter Dobing was a mainstay and club captain at Stoke City between 1963-73. After arriving from Manchester City he made 307 appearances for the Potters and scored an impressive 83 goals from the inside forward position.

Willie Stevenson was signed
by Tony Waddington from
Liverpool in 1967. Playing
as a wing-half he made
94 appearances for the
club before moving on to
Tranmere Rovers.

Peter Dobing has to be restrained by his team-mates after losing his cool. Dobing was a mainstay at the
club throughout the 1960s and early 70s. In fact he ended his career with the Potters and retired from
football in 1973 after playing 307 first team games.

Stoke City's achievements in the 1970s were largely down to a group of skilful and loyal players who gave their all for the club. In return they were loved and respected by the fans. Names such as Peter Dobing, Gordon Banks and Terry Conroy stir up incredible memories in the mind's of Stoke supporters.

Two of Stoke City's goalkeeping greats are seen here shaking hands. Gordon Banks stayed at Stoke until he tragically lost the use of one of his eyes after a car accident in 1974. His replacement Peter Shilton also came from Leicester City and made 110 appearances before moving on to Nottingham Forest.

Sean Haslegrave rises to head the ball. Haslegrave was another product of Stoke's successful youth system. After 113 league appearances, he was transferred to Nottingham Forest in 1976.

Harry Burrows chases a loose ball during a match against Arsenal in 1970. This was an amazing game where Stoke managed to beat Arsenal 5-0. Burrows joined from Aston Villa in 1964 and went on to play 245 league games as a winger.

A rare picture showing two of Stoke and England's most outstanding goalkeepers in action at the same time. Banks played 194 games for Stoke, Shilton was brought in as his replacement for a world-record £325,000 in November 1974.

Arsenal's Frank McLintock is seen
here enjoying a post-match glass of
champagne to celebrate Arsenal's
victory over Stoke in the F.A Cup
semi-final in 1971/72.

In 1970/71 and 1971/72 seasons Stoke came excruciatingly close to capturing the F.A Cup. However they had the misfortune to face Arsenal in the semi-final of the F.A Cup in two successive years. In the first encounter, Stoke drew 2-2 at Hillsborough but Arsenal went on to win the replay by 2-0 at Villa Park.

A dejected Alan Bloor trudges off the Villa Park pitch after Stoke suffered a 2-0 defeat signalling the end of their cup dreams for another season. The first leg at Hillsborough ended in a draw but Stoke were unfortunately outplayed in the return leg of the F.A Cup semi-final.

1972 League Cup-Final

On March 4 1972, Stoke captured the League Cup with a thrilling 2-1 victory over Chelsea in front of a packed Wembley Stadium. It was the first major trophy that Stoke City had obtained during their long history, giving fans a perfect excuse for celebration.

The streets of Stoke-on-Trent were flooded with well-wishers and the team was granted a hero's welcome on their return. Over 250,000 people came along to see the victorious players. An open top bus was commandeered specifically for the occasion and the League Cup was proudly displayed around the town.

Peter Dobing and Gordon Banks review just a few of the many letters of congratulation that the team received after their victorious League Cup run in 1972. At the time Stoke were one of the most feared cup teams around.

Pictured here in September 1972 are Stoke City players and Chairman Mr Albert Henshall showing off the mugs that were manufactured to commemorate the League Cup win over Chelsea in 1972.

Stoke City fans like those pictured here had an incredible day out on March 4 1972. With one of the world-famous Twin Towers of Wembley Stadium behind them, Stoke fans are seen making the most of a fantastic occasion.

Just some of the huge crowd that made the trip to Wembley to see Stoke battle Chelsea in the League Cup final in 1972.

Tony Waddington talks tactics with his captain Peter Dobing as Stoke City and Chelsea make their way on to the Wembley pitch prior to the match.

This fantastic picture illustrates the sheer scale of the legendary Wembley Stadium. Over 40,000 Stoke supporters were present to see their team's famous 2-1 victory over Chelsea.

Stoke City players Mike Pejic, Gordon Banks and Jackie Marsh seen in action during the 1972 League Cup final. Together they manage to prevent a Chelsea goal.

As the Chelsea wall lines up in order to defend a Stoke City free-kick, the enormous crowd inside Wembley Stadium hold their breaths in anticipation. The ground was the scene of Stoke's greatest triumph and to date the only major trophy captured during the club's long and illustrious history.

Alan Bloor and Mike Pejic are pictured here in action against Chelsea. Both of these players came through the youth system at Stoke and went on to have fantastic careers. Pejic was one of the most competitive players to ever wear the red and white strip. He went on to win four full England caps before being sold to Everton after making 336 appearances.

With arms raised, Jimmy Greenhoff celebrates Terry Conroy's goal against Chelsea's keeper Peter Bonetti during the League Cup final in 1972.

Jimmy Greenhoff was idolised by the Stoke faithful for his almost telepathic understanding with Alan Hudson and John Ritchie. He was a member of the Stoke City squad that took part in the 1972 League Cup final. Greenhoff scored 97 goals in 378 league games before joining Manchester United in 1976 for £120,000.

Peter Dobing, Stoke City's victorious captain lifts the League Cup in salute to the many thousands of travelling fans who had made the long trip from Stoke to Wembley.

Stoke City players proudly hold the League Cup aloft after their superb 2-1 victory in 1972.

Terry Conroy, Jackie Marsh, Gordon Banks, Peter Dobing and Mike Pejic begin to wind down in the bath with a well-deserved bottle of beer at the conclusion of the League Cup Final. All of the players garnered huge respect and admiration from the Stoke public for both their professionalism and considerable skill.

Just part of the throng of Stoke City fans who made the journey to Wembley and turned the stadium into a sea of red and white on the day.

This photograph perfectly demonstrates the huge show of affection Stoke received on their return to the Potteries after the tremendous League Cup victory.

Stoke City's fans took to the streets in order to welcome home their conquering heroes in 1972. Members of the cup-winning team sit on top of a specially organised bus to display the trophy they had won.

Tony Waddington and the Stoke City team sit proudly on top of the bus used to transport the team around the Potteries to let the fans show their appreciation for the achievements Stoke City made in winning the Cup.

Peter Dobing leads the Stoke City team out on to the pitch proudly holding the League Cup in his right hand and the ball in the other. This was the team's first opportunity to show their trophy in front of a home crowd.

Stoke City's traditional Loving cup ceremony was held on their first home game of the season against Liverpool. Liverpool's chairman Mr John W.Smith drinks champagne from the cup watched by his counterpart at Stoke Mr Albert Henshall.

Inspecting the Victoria Ground pitch are Keith Northwood (left) and Len Parton.

Eric Skeels, Geoff Hurst and Terry Smith leave the coach which brought them back from a training session. Smith made only 2 appearances for the club between 1970-72 before moving to Australia to join Brisbane City.

Stoke's players enjoying a jog in the Potteries sunshine in August 1974. Among those seen here are Jackie Marsh, Geoff Hurst and John Ritchie.

Stoke City's senior players including Geoff Hurst, Jimmy Greenhoff and John Ritchie line up to have their photographs taken prior to the 1974/75 season.

A tough training session is taking place in the countryside surrounding Stoke-on-Trent in 1973.

John Mahoney and John Ritchie combine here to score the goal which ensured Stoke obtained a draw in this game with Chelsea. John Mahoney made 282 league appearances for the club and scored 25 goals from midfield before being transferred to Middlesbrough in 1977.

Stoke City footballers are pictured giving a demonstration of heading tennis at the North Staffordshire Physically Handicapped Society at Trentham Gardens. In the picture, John Ritchie heads over to Alan Dodd. Dodd had two spells with the club after coming up through the youth system. He made 372 league appearances before being transferred to Wolves in 1982.

Peter Dobing leads out the Stoke City reserve team followed by Mike McDonald. McDonald was signed from Clydebank in 1972 but only made 5 first team appearances before returning to Scotland with Hibernian in 1974.

A capacity crowd at Derby County's Baseball Ground looks on as a Stoke player attempts to shield the ball from Kevin Hector of Derby County. The match ended in a 1-1 draw in June 1974.

Republic of Ireland winger Terry Conroy battling back to fitness after yet another cartilage operation. In this pre-season match he showed glimpses of the form that led him to 271 Stoke City league appearances between 1967-79, after he arrived from Glentoran in Northern Ireland.

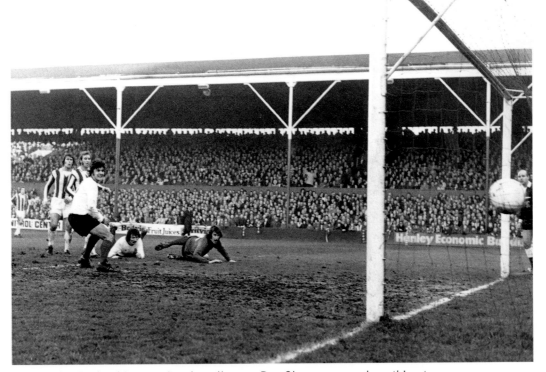

Liverpool's England international goalkeeper Ray Clemence can do nothing to prevent Stoke City scoring when the clubs met at the Victoria Ground on the 19 January 1974. The match ended in a 1-1 draw.

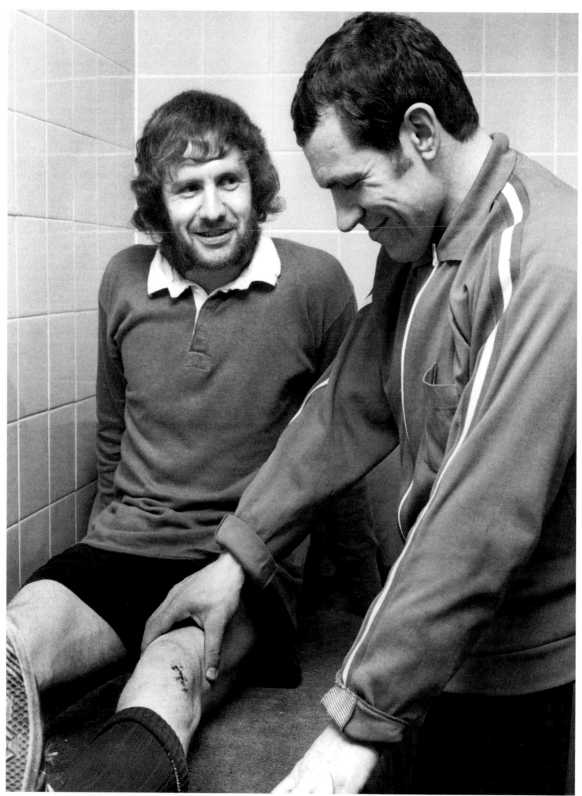

Stoke City winger Terry Conroy receives treatment from physiotherapist Mike Allen on his injured knee. Although his career was disrupted by injury, Conroy still managed 271 league games and became a firm favourite with the club's fans.

Stoke City hopefuls, from left to right are: Stefan Fenwick, Gary Haynes, Mick Smith, Garth Crooks, Martin Brown and Bryan Jones.

Alan Hudson attempts to block a cross by the Arsenal full-back during Stoke's 2-0 defeat at Highbury in 1976. Hudson was a player of considerable vision and skill. He did a great job for Stoke and made 105 appearances in his first spell at the club. He then left Stoke to join Arsenal before moving to America to play for the Seattle Sounders before returning to Stoke in 1983.

Denis Smith, Everton's Bob Latchford and Stoke goalkeeper John Farmer fight for the ball at Goodison Park. The game ended in a 2-1 defeat for Stoke.

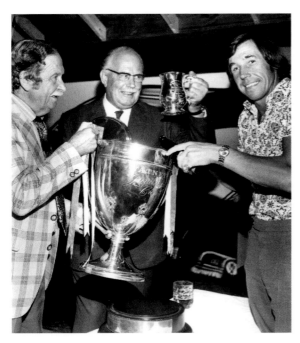

In a happy mood, Gordon Banks and Stoke City chairman Albert Henshall with the Watney Cup. The club were presented with a replica of the cup as they were the last team to win the competition before it ceased.

Tony Waddington signed Peter Shilton in order to replace Gordon Banks. At the time, the amount paid for Shilton was a world-record fee for a goalkeeper. But the £325,000 transfer fee soon looked like money well spent as Shilton went on to prove his undoubted class.

David Goodwin runs out on to the pitch. Goodwin came through the club's famous youth system but only managed 26 games and 3 goals before leaving for Mansfield Town in 1978.

Manchester United fans are keenly examined by the police ahead of their clubs clash with Stoke City.

Just a few of the items taken by the police at the turnstiles of the Victoria Ground before the notorious match against Manchester United in April 1974.

Mounted police try to keep the crowds under control at the Victoria Ground. Despite their valiant efforts, Manchester United fans left a trail of destruction in their wake.

Although many fights broke out after the game, police managed to control rival sets of fans during the match. In total 17 people were arrested and police seized a hoard of weapons including knives, hammers and baseball bats.

Extra police officers were drafted in for the Stoke City v Manchester United clash, however, a large number of shops and pubs suffered damage in the aftermath of the game.

Stoke City fans show their support for the club after the game against Manchester United in 1974.

The Stoke City team took part in a football quiz against members of the Stoke City Social Club. Left to right are: John Mahoney (captain), Denis Smith, Alan A'Court and John Ritchie.

Terry Conroy gets some
unexpected news and
his fellow team mate
Jimmy Greenhoff
winces in sympathy.

Newcastle and England international Malcolm MacDonald attempts to take the ball past a Stoke City
defender during the teams' 2-2 draw at the Victoria Ground in October 1974.

John Mahoney is seen here dribbling through the Blackburn Rovers defence in 1974.

Peter Bonetti, the Chelsea goalkeeper picks the ball out of the net after Stoke City scored a penalty during the 3-0 victory that Stoke achieved in April 1975.

Geoff Hurst does what he does best by putting the ball into the back of the net when Stoke played Newcastle in 1975.

The latter part of the 1970s were not kind on Stoke City. A storm blew off part of the Butler Street Stand roof in January 1976. This damage cost £250,000 to repair and precipitated the financial troubles which saw players such as Alan Hudson, Mike Pejic and Jimmy Greenhoff sold off in order to cover the debt.

A smiling Garth Crooks takes to the field before a Stoke City game at the Victoria Ground.

Jimmy Greenhoff gives the thumbs up to celebrate a victory. After his impressive 8-year career at Stoke, Greenhoff was snapped up by Manchester United.

The front cover for the programme commemorating the 5th Round F.A Cup tie against Sunderland in 1976. Sunderland eventually won the game 2-1 and knocked Stoke City out of the Cup.

Terry Conroy throws a body-swerve in order to take the ball past a fallen defender.

Alan Hudson of Stoke City and Steve Powell of Derby County battle for the ball when the two teams clashed in October 1976. Stoke lost this game at home 1-0.

Chapter 4
1975-80

The latter end of the 1970s proved to be a tough time for both the club and the fans. After tasting so much success earlier on in the decade, Stoke City were just not able to push on and really challenge for league and Cup titles.

When the roof of the Butler Street Stand blew off in January 1976 it brought bad tidings for Stoke. The damage cost over £250,000 to repair and this started off a run of financial problems that led to many of the players being sacrificed in order to keep Stoke City FC above water.

Amongst those sold off were Hudson, Pejic and Greenhoff. The team could not stand the impact of such losses and they were relegated at the end of 1976/77. Tony Waddington was another unfortunate casualty as his long and successful reign came to an end. George Eastham took over the running of the club for a short time but he left the club after the 1977/78 season.

Results picked up after Alan Durban was recruited as manager from Shrewsbury Town. He brought in a new sense of discipline and fitness that spread throughout the team. Along with Howard Kendall, promotion back to Division One was clinched on the final day of the 1978/79 season thanks to a late goal from Paul Richardson at Notts County.

This wonderful picture shows Geoff Scott who played 78 games in defence for Stoke between 1977-80 and Garth Crooks.

Stoke City's Garth Crooks shows the technique that made him a firm favourite with the Potteries' public. Crooks was a product of the youth system at Stoke and went on to play for both Tottenham Hotspur and England.

A new-look Stoke City first-team squad is pictured here in preparation for the 1977/78 season. Back row (left to right) are Terry Conroy, Paul Richardson, Alan Dodd, Danny Bowers Roger Jones, Alec Lindsay, Alan Bloor, Viv Busby and Geoff Scott. At the front are Garth Crooks, David Gregory, Howard Kendall, Denis Smith, Jeff Cook, Des Backos, John Marsh and Steve Waddington (kneeling).

All the traditional goodwill was evident at the Loving Cup ceremony in the Stoke City boardroom before the first home game of the season. Mr Sandy Chubb drinks from the cup. The opponents on the day were Coventry City and Stoke won the game 3-2.

A lone fan looks on as Stoke City's Victoria Ground is covered in snow. It is a beautiful scene but this fan is probably worrying about the chances of seeing his team in action.

Some of Stoke City's ground staff and apprentices are pictured here working hard to try and get the Victoria Ground to a playable state in February 1979.

Stoke's players train on a cold, winters day.

Stoke City youngsters clear the snow away from the Victoria Ground in March 1979. This kind of concerted effort improved team spirit amongst the players.

Paul Randall is seen here in action for Stoke City. He was signed from Bristol Rovers in 1978 and made 46 league appearances as a striker, scoring 7 goals before returning to the Bristol club in 1981.

Garth Crooks finds himself inside the Coventry City net after scoring another goal for Stoke City. A strewn Coventry defender looks on despairingly.

Howard Kendall is carried off the pitch by a Stoke physiotherapist and also the referee during the game against Luton in 1979.

Howard Kendall is treated by physiotherapist Mike Allen as manager Alan Durban cheers on his team from the sidelines. Kendall joined the club from Birmingham in 1977 and stayed for two years, clocking up 82 games and 9 goals from his position in midfield.

Stoke City's number 9 leaps in the air with joy as he celebrates a goal for the club.

A scrum of Stoke City players including Garth Crooks and Mike Doyle celebrate a goal.

The Coventry City goalkeeper dives despairingly to his left but can do nothing to prevent the shot flying past him and into the net. This was a high-scoring game that ended in a 3-2 Stoke victory.

Footballing Maestro Sir Stanley Matthews back at the Victoria Ground discusses details with manager Alan Durban about a competition to be held in Malta, which Stoke City competed in. Also pictured is Alan Busby of Paro International, representing the organisers of the competition.

Stoke-on-Trent's Lord Mayor greets the Republic of Ireland team before a friendly match at Stoke City's Victoria Ground.

A policeman examines the stands in preparation for Stoke City's next home match. These vantage points proved invaluable when it came to identifying potential troublemakers.

The Victoria Ground as seen from the police control centre. It gave the officers dealing with crowd trouble at matches a panoramic view of the whole ground. Looking out from its toughened glass windows are, left to right, club chairman Mr Tom Degg, Staffordshire's Chief Constable Mr Charles Kelly, Assistant Chief Constable Mr Ken Gibson and Constable Graham (seated).

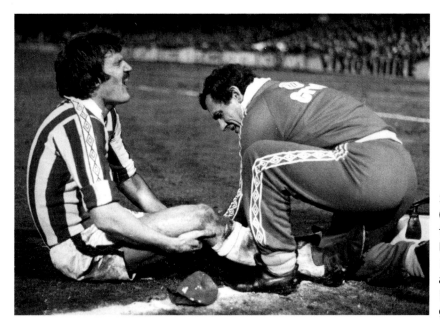

Stoke City's Brendan O'Callaghan receives treatment on an injured knee from physiotherapist Mike Allen just minutes after scoring against Preston to equalise the game for Stoke.

Garth Crooks puts away a penalty against Tottenham in 1979. So impressed were Spurs by Crooks's performance that they snapped him up just a few months later.

The opposition goalkeeper dives despairingly in an attempt to save a shot from Stoke City.

Geoff Scott is seen here in action for Stoke City in July 1979. Scott was signed from Highgate United in 1977 and made 78 appearances before being sold to Leicester City in 1986.

The Wolves goalkeeper plucks the ball out of the air against Stoke City. The game ended in a 1-0 loss for the Potters.

In an attempt to prevent the tide of hooliganism sweeping the nation this type of fencing became an all too common site at football grounds during the late 1970s and early 1980s.

Lined up are members of Stoke City FC for the 1977/78 season.

Howard Kendall conducts a training session at Stoke City's training ground in 1979. Kendall joined the club from Birmingham in 1977 and featured both as a player and a coach.

Garth Crooks beats his man as he charges down the wing against Crystal Palace in September 1976. The game ended in a defeat for Stoke City.

Terry Conroy of Stoke City battles with Arsenal goalkeeper Bob Wilson as John Ritchie and Frank McLintoch look on. Arsenal's relationship with Stoke City was an intensely interesting one. The clubs met on many occasions during the 1970s, most notably the two F.A Cup semi-final defeats which the Gunners inflicted on Stoke in consecutive seasons.

Sammy Irvine signed for Stoke from Shrewsbury Town in 1978 and made 67 league appearances in mid-field before his career was unfortunately cut short by injury.

Stoke City's players salute their fans after the final league match of the 1978/79 season. The match against Newcastle ended in a draw. Manager Alan Durban is to the left with Mike Doyle, while Denis Smith gets attention from eager young fans.

Facts and Statistics

This section follows Stoke City's progress through the 60s and 70s in league tables. Also included are some general facts and statistics about the Potters and their players.

Discover the most capped player, top goalscorer and many more facts about your favourite team in the 60s and 70s.

Stanley Matthews in training with the Stoke City Squad during the 60s.

LEAGUE TABLES 1960-61

SECOND DIVISION

		P	W	D	L	F	A	Pts
1.	Ipswich	42	26	7	9	100	55	59
2.	Sheffield United	42	26	6	10	81	51	58
3.	Liverpool	42	21	10	11	87	58	52
4.	Norwich	42	20	9	13	70	53	49
5.	Middlesbrough	42	18	12	12	83	74	48
6.	Sunderland	42	17	13	12	75	60	47
7.	Swansea	42	18	11	13	77	73	47
8.	Southampton	42	18	8	16	84	81	44
9.	Scunthorpe	42	14	15	13	69	64	43
10.	Charlton Athletic	42	16	11	15	97	91	43
11.	Plymouth	42	17	8	17	81	82	42
12.	Derby	42	15	10	17	80	80	40
13.	Luton	42	15	9	18	71	70	39
14.	Leeds	42	14	10	18	75	83	38
15.	Rotherham	42	12	13	17	65	64	37
16.	Brighton	42	14	9	19	61	75	37
17.	Bristol Rovers	42	15	7	20	73	92	37
18.	**Stoke**	**42**	**12**	**12**	**18**	**51**	**59**	**36**
19.	Leyton Orient	42	14	8	20	55	78	36
20.	Huddersfield	42	13	9	20	62	71	35
21.	Portsmouth	42	11	11	20	64	91	33
22.	Lincoln	42	8	8	26	48	95	24

LEAGUE TABLES 1961-62

SECOND DIVISION

		P	W	D	L	F	A	Pts
1.	Liverpool	42	27	8	7	99	43	62
2.	Leyton Orient	42	22	10	10	69	40	54
3.	Sunderland	42	22	9	11	85	50	53
4.	Scunthorpe	42	21	7	14	86	71	49
5.	Plymouth	42	19	8	15	75	75	46
6.	Southampton	42	18	9	15	77	62	45
7.	Huddersfield	42	16	12	14	67	59	44
8.	**Stoke**	**42**	**17**	**8**	**17**	**55**	**57**	**42**
9.	Rotherham	42	16	9	17	70	76	41
10.	Preston	42	15	10	17	55	57	40
11.	Newcastle	42	15	9	18	64	58	39
12.	Middlesbrough	42	16	7	19	76	72	39
13.	Luton	42	17	5	20	69	71	39
14.	Walsall	42	14	11	17	70	75	39
15.	Charlton	42	15	9	18	69	75	39
16.	Derby	42	14	11	17	68	75	39
17.	Norwich	42	14	11	17	61	70	39
18.	Bury	42	17	5	20	52	76	39
19.	Leeds	42	12	12	18	50	61	36
20.	Swansea	42	12	12	18	61	83	36
21.	Bristol Rovers	42	13	7	22	53	81	33
22.	Brighton	42	10	11	21	42	86	31

LEAGUE TABLES 1962-63

SECOND DIVISION

		P	W	D	L	F	A	Pts
1.	**Stoke**	**42**	**20**	**13**	**9**	**73**	**50**	**53**
2.	Chelsea	42	24	4	14	81	42	52
3.	Sunderland	42	20	12	10	84	55	52
4.	Middlesbrough	42	20	9	13	86	85	49
5.	Leeds	42	19	10	13	79	53	48
6.	Huddersfield	42	17	14	11	63	50	48
7.	Newcastle	42	18	11	13	79	59	47
8.	Bury	42	18	11	13	51	47	47
9.	Scunthorpe	42	16	12	14	57	59	44
10.	Cardiff	42	18	7	17	83	73	43
11.	Southampton	42	17	8	17	72	67	42
12.	Plymouth	42	15	12	15	76	73	42
13.	Norwich	42	17	8	17	80	79	42
14.	Rotherham	42	17	6	19	67	74	40
15.	Swansea	42	15	9	18	51	72	39
16.	Portsmouth	42	13	11	18	63	79	37
17.	Preston	42	13	11	18	59	74	37
18.	Derby	42	12	12	18	61	72	36
19.	Grimsby	42	11	13	18	55	66	35
20.	Charlton	42	13	5	24	62	94	31
21.	Walsall	42	11	9	22	53	89	31
22.	Luton	42	11	7	24	61	84	29

LEAGUE TABLES 1963-64

FIRST DIVISION

		P	W	D	L	F	A	Pts
1.	Liverpool	42	26	5	11	92	45	57
2.	Man United	42	23	7	12	90	62	53
3.	Everton	42	21	10	11	84	64	52
4.	Tottenham	42	22	7	13	97	81	51
5.	Chelsea	42	20	10	12	72	56	50
6.	Sheffield Wed	42	19	11	12	84	67	49
7.	Blackburn	42	18	10	14	89	65	46
8.	Arsenal	42	17	11	14	90	82	45
9.	Burnley	42	17	10	15	71	64	44
10.	WBA	42	16	11	15	70	61	43
11.	Leicester	42	16	11	15	61	58	43
12.	Sheffield United	42	16	11	15	61	64	43
13.	Nottm Forest	42	16	9	17	64	68	41
14.	West Ham	42	14	12	16	69	74	40
15.	Fulham	42	13	13	16	58	65	39
16.	Wolves	42	12	15	15	70	80	39
17.	**Stoke**	**42**	**14**	**10**	**18**	**77**	**78**	**38**
18.	Blackpool	42	13	9	20	52	73	35
19.	Aston Villa	42	11	12	19	62	71	34
20.	Birmingham	42	11	7	24	54	92	29
21.	Bolton	42	10	8	24	48	80	28
22.	Ipswich	42	9	7	26	56	121	25

LEAGUE TABLES 1964-65

FIRST DIVISION

		P	W	D	L	F	A	Pts
1.	Man United	42	26	9	7	89	39	61
2.	Leeds	42	26	9	7	83	52	61
3.	Chelsea	42	24	8	10	89	54	56
4.	Everton	42	17	15	10	69	60	49
5.	Nottm Forest	42	17	13	12	71	67	47
6.	Tottenham	42	19	7	16	87	71	45
7.	Liverpool	42	17	10	15	67	73	44
8.	Sheffield Wed	42	16	11	15	57	55	43
9.	West Ham	42	19	4	19	82	71	42
10.	Blackburn	42	16	10	16	83	79	42
11.	**Stoke**	**42**	**16**	**10**	**16**	**67**	**66**	**42**
12.	Burnley	42	16	10	16	70	70	42
13.	Arsenal	42	17	7	18	69	75	41
14.	WBA	42	13	13	16	70	65	39
15.	Sunderland	42	14	9	19	64	74	37
16.	Aston Villa	42	16	5	21	57	82	37
17.	Blackpool	42	12	11	19	67	78	35
18.	Leicester	42	11	13	18	69	85	35
19.	Sheffield United	42	12	11	19	50	64	35
20.	Fulham	42	11	12	19	60	78	34
21.	Wolves	42	13	4	25	59	89	30
22.	Birmingham	42	8	11	23	64	96	27

LEAGUE TABLES 1965-66

FIRST DIVISION

		P	W	D	L	F	A	Pts
1.	Liverpool	42	26	9	7	79	34	61
2.	Leeds	42	23	9	10	79	38	55
3.	Burnley	42	24	7	11	79	47	55
4.	Man United	42	18	15	9	84	59	51
5.	Chelsea	42	22	7	13	65	53	51
6.	WBA	42	19	12	11	91	69	50
7.	Leicester	42	21	7	14	80	65	49
8.	Tottenham	42	16	12	14	75	66	44
9.	Sheffield United	42	16	11	15	56	59	43
10.	**Stoke**	**42**	**15**	**12**	**15**	**65**	**64**	**42**
11.	Everton	42	15	11	16	56	62	41
12.	West Ham	42	15	9	18	70	83	39
13.	Blackpool	42	14	9	19	55	65	37
14.	Arsenal	42	12	13	17	62	75	37
15.	Newcastle	42	14	9	19	50	63	37
16.	Aston Villa	42	15	6	21	69	80	36
17.	Sheffield Wed	42	14	8	20	56	66	36
18.	Nottm Forest	42	14	8	20	56	72	36
19.	Sunderland	42	14	8	20	51	72	36
20.	Fulham	42	14	7	21	67	85	35
21.	Northampton	42	10	13	19	55	92	33
22.	Blackburn	42	8	4	30	57	88	20

LEAGUE TABLES 1966-67

FIRST DIVISION

		P	W	D	L	F	A	Pts
1.	Man United	42	24	12	6	84	45	60
2.	Nottm Forest	42	23	10	9	64	41	56
3.	Tottenham	42	24	8	10	71	48	56
4.	Leeds	42	22	11	9	62	42	55
5.	Liverpool	42	19	13	10	64	47	51
6.	Everton	42	19	10	13	65	46	48
7.	Arsenal	42	16	14	12	58	47	46
8.	Leicester	42	18	8	16	78	71	44
9.	Chelsea	42	15	14	13	67	62	44
10.	Sheffield United	42	16	10	16	52	59	42
11.	Sheffield Wed	42	14	13	15	56	47	41
12.	**Stoke**	**42**	**17**	**7**	**18**	**63**	**58**	**41**
13.	WBA	42	16	7	19	77	73	39
14.	Burnley	42	15	9	18	66	76	39
15.	Man City	42	12	15	15	43	52	39
16.	West Ham	42	14	8	20	80	84	36
17.	Sunderland	42	14	8	20	58	72	36
18.	Fulham	42	11	12	19	71	83	34
19.	Southampton	42	14	6	22	74	92	34
20.	Newcastle	42	12	9	21	39	81	33
21.	Aston Villa	42	11	7	24	54	85	29
22.	Blackpool	42	6	9	27	41	76	21

LEAGUE TABLES 1967-68

FIRST DIVISION

		P	W	D	L	F	A	Pts
1.	Man City	42	26	6	10	86	43	58
2.	Man United	42	24	8	10	89	55	56
3.	Liverpool	42	22	11	9	71	40	55
4.	Leeds	42	22	9	11	71	41	53
5.	Everton	42	23	6	13	67	40	52
6.	Chelsea	42	18	12	12	62	68	48
7.	Tottenham	42	19	9	14	70	59	47
8.	WBA	42	17	12	13	75	62	46
9.	Arsenal	42	17	10	15	60	56	44
10.	Newcastle	42	13	15	14	54	67	41
11.	Nottm Forest	42	14	11	17	52	64	39
12.	West Ham	42	14	10	18	73	69	38
13.	Leicester	42	13	12	17	64	69	38
14.	Burnley	42	14	10	18	64	71	38
15.	Sunderland	42	13	11	18	51	61	37
16.	Southampton	42	13	11	18	66	83	37
17.	Wolves	42	14	8	20	66	75	36
18.	**Stoke**	**42**	**14**	**7**	**21**	**50**	**73**	**35**
19.	Sheffield Wed	42	11	12	19	51	63	34
20.	Coventry	42	9	15	18	51	71	33
21.	Sheffield United	42	11	10	21	49	70	32
22.	Fulham	42	10	7	25	56	98	27

LEAGUE TABLES 1968-69

FIRST DIVISION

		P	W	D	L	F	A	Pts
1.	Leeds	42	27	13	2	66	26	67
2.	Liverpool	42	25	11	6	63	24	61
3.	Everton	42	21	15	6	77	36	57
4.	Arsenal	42	22	12	8	56	27	56
5.	Chelsea	42	20	10	12	73	53	50
6.	Tottenham	42	14	17	11	61	51	45
7.	Southampton	42	16	13	13	57	48	45
8.	West Ham	42	13	18	11	66	50	44
9.	Newcastle	42	15	14	13	61	55	44
10.	WBA	42	16	11	15	64	67	43
11.	Man United	42	15	12	15	57	53	42
12.	Ipswich	42	15	11	16	59	60	41
13.	Man City	42	15	10	17	64	55	40
14.	Burnley	42	15	9	18	55	82	39
15.	Sheffield Wed	42	10	16	16	41	54	36
16.	Wolves	42	10	15	17	41	58	35
17.	Sunderland	42	11	12	19	43	67	34
18.	Nottm Forest	42	10	13	19	45	57	33
19.	**Stoke**	**42**	**9**	**15**	**18**	**40**	**63**	**33**
20.	Coventry	42	10	11	21	46	64	31
21.	Leicester	42	9	12	21	39	68	30
22.	QPR	42	4	10	28	39	95	18

LEAGUE TABLES 1969-70

FIRST DIVISION

		P	W	D	L	F	A	Pts
1.	Everton	42	29	8	5	72	34	66
2.	Leeds	42	21	15	6	84	49	57
3.	Chelsea	42	21	13	8	70	50	55
4.	Derby	42	22	9	11	64	37	53
5.	Liverpool	42	20	11	11	65	42	51
6.	Coventry	42	19	11	12	58	48	49
7.	Newcastle	42	17	13	12	57	35	47
8.	Man United	42	14	17	11	66	61	45
9.	**Stoke**	**42**	**15**	**15**	**12**	**56**	**52**	**45**
10.	Man City	42	16	11	15	55	48	43
11.	Tottenham	42	17	9	16	54	55	43
12.	Arsenal	42	12	18	12	51	49	42
13.	Wolves	42	12	16	14	55	57	40
14.	Burnley	42	12	15	15	56	61	39
15.	Nottm Forest	42	10	18	14	50	71	38
16.	WBA	42	14	9	19	58	66	37
17.	West Ham	42	12	12	18	51	60	36
18.	Ipswich	42	10	11	21	40	63	31
19.	Southampton	42	6	17	19	46	67	29
20.	Crystal Palace	42	6	15	21	34	68	27
21.	Sunderland	42	6	14	22	30	68	26
22.	Sheffield Wed	42	8	9	25	40	71	25

LEAGUE TABLES 1970-71

FIRST DIVISION

		P	W	D	L	F	A	Pts
1.	Arsenal	42	29	7	6	71	29	65
2.	Leeds	42	27	10	5	72	30	64
3.	Tottenham	42	19	14	9	54	33	52
4.	Wolves	42	22	8	12	64	54	52
5.	Liverpool	42	17	17	8	42	24	51
6.	Chelsea	42	18	15	9	52	42	51
7.	Southampton	42	17	12	13	56	44	46
8.	Man United	42	16	11	15	65	66	43
9.	Derby	42	16	10	16	56	54	42
10.	Coventry	42	16	10	16	37	38	42
11.	Man City	42	12	17	13	47	42	41
12.	Newcastle	42	14	13	15	44	46	41
13.	**Stoke**	**42**	**12**	**13**	**17**	**44**	**48**	**37**
14.	Everton	42	12	13	17	54	60	37
15.	Huddersfield	42	11	14	17	40	49	36
16.	Nottm Forest	42	14	8	20	42	61	36
17.	WBA	42	10	15	17	58	75	35
18.	Crystal Palace	42	12	11	19	39	57	35
19.	Ipswich	42	12	10	20	42	48	34
20.	West Ham	42	10	14	18	47	60	34
21.	Burnley	42	7	13	22	29	63	27
22.	Blackpool	42	4	15	23	34	66	23

LEAGUE TABLES 1971-72

FIRST DIVISION

		P	W	D	L	F	A	Pts
1.	Derby	42	24	10	8	69	33	58
2.	Leeds	42	24	9	9	73	31	57
3.	Liverpool	42	24	9	9	64	30	57
4.	Man City	42	23	11	8	77	45	57
5.	Arsenal	42	22	8	12	58	40	52
6.	Tottenham	42	19	13	10	63	42	51
7.	Chelsea	42	18	12	12	58	49	48
8.	Man United	42	19	10	13	69	61	48
9.	Wolves	42	18	11	13	65	57	47
10.	Sheffield United	42	17	11	13	61	60	46
11.	Newcastle	42	15	11	16	49	52	41
12.	Leicester	42	13	13	16	41	46	39
13.	Ipswich	42	12	16	15	39	53	38
14.	West Ham	42	12	12	18	47	51	36
15.	Everton	42	9	18	15	37	48	36
16.	WBA	42	12	11	19	42	54	35
17.	**Stoke**	**42**	**10**	**15**	**17**	**39**	**56**	**35**
18.	Coventry	42	9	15	18	44	67	33
19.	Southampton	42	12	7	23	52	80	31
20.	Crystal Palace	42	8	13	21	39	65	29
21.	Nottm Forest	42	8	9	25	47	81	25
22.	Huddersfield	42	6	13	23	27	59	25

LEAGUE TABLES 1972-73

FIRST DIVISION

		P	W	D	L	F	A	Pts
1.	Liverpool	42	25	10	6	72	42	60
2.	Arsenal	42	23	11	8	57	43	57
3.	Leeds	42	21	11	10	77	45	53
4.	Ipswich	42	17	14	11	55	45	48
5.	Wolves	42	18	11	13	66	54	47
6.	West Ham	42	17	12	13	67	53	46
7.	Derby	42	19	8	15	56	54	46
8.	Tottenham	42	16	13	13	58	48	45
9.	Newcastle	42	16	13	13	60	51	45
10.	Birmingham	42	15	12	15	53	54	42
11.	Man City	42	15	11	16	57	60	41
12.	Chelsea	42	13	14	15	49	51	40
13.	Southampton	42	11	18	13	47	52	40
14.	Sheffield Wed	42	15	10	17	51	59	40
15.	**Stoke**	**42**	**14**	**10**	**18**	**61**	**56**	**38**
16.	Leicester	42	10	17	15	40	46	37
17.	Everton	42	13	11	18	41	49	37
18.	Man United	42	12	13	17	44	60	37
19.	Coventry	42	13	9	20	40	55	35
20.	Norwich	42	11	10	21	36	63	32
21.	Crystal Palace	42	9	12	21	41	58	30
22.	WBA	42	9	10	23	38	62	28

LEAGUE TABLES 1973-74

FIRST DIVISION

		P	W	D	L	F	A	Pts
1.	Leeds	42	24	14	4	66	31	62
2.	Liverpool	42	22	13	7	52	31	57
3.	Derby	42	17	14	11	52	42	48
4.	Ipswich	42	18	11	13	67	58	47
5.	**Stoke**	**42**	**15**	**16**	**11**	**54**	**42**	**46**
6.	Burnley	42	16	14	12	56	53	46
7.	Everton	42	16	12	14	50	48	44
8.	QPR	42	13	17	12	56	52	43
9.	Leicester	42	13	16	13	51	41	42
10.	Arsenal	42	14	14	14	49	51	42
11.	Tottenham	42	14	14	14	45	50	42
12.	Wolves	42	13	15	14	49	49	41
13.	Sheffield United	42	14	12	16	44	49	40
14.	Man City	42	14	12	16	39	46	40
15.	Newcastle	42	13	12	17	49	48	38
16.	Coventry	42	14	10	18	43	54	38
17.	Chelsea	42	12	13	17	56	60	37
18.	West Ham	42	11	15	16	55	60	37
19.	Birmingham	42	12	13	17	52	64	37
20.	Southampton	42	11	14	17	47	68	36
21.	Man United	42	10	12	20	38	48	32
22.	Norwich	42	7	15	20	37	62	29

LEAGUE TABLES 1974-75

FIRST DIVISION

		P	W	D	L	F	A	Pts
1.	Derby	42	21	11	10	67	49	53
2.	Liverpool	42	20	11	11	60	39	51
3.	Ipswich	42	23	5	14	66	44	51
4.	Everton	42	16	18	8	56	42	50
5.	**Stoke**	**42**	**17**	**15**	**10**	**64**	**48**	**49**
6.	Sheffield United	42	18	13	11	58	51	49
7.	Middlesbrough	42	18	12	12	54	40	48
8.	Man City	42	18	10	14	54	54	46
9.	Leeds	42	16	13	13	57	49	45
10.	Burnley	42	17	11	14	68	67	45
11.	QPR	42	16	10	16	54	54	42
12.	Wolverhampton	42	14	11	17	57	54	39
13.	West Ham	42	13	13	16	58	59	39
14.	Coventry	42	12	15	15	51	62	39
15.	Newcastle	42	15	9	18	59	72	39
16.	Arsenal	42	13	11	18	47	49	37
17.	Birmingham	42	14	9	19	53	61	37
18.	Leicester	42	12	12	18	46	60	36
19.	Tottenham	42	13	8	21	52	63	34
20.	Luton	42	11	11	20	47	65	33
21.	Chelsea	42	9	15	18	42	72	33
22.	Carlisle	42	12	5	25	43	59	29

LEAGUE TABLES 1975-76

FIRST DIVISION

		P	W	D	L	F	A	Pts
1.	Liverpool	42	23	14	5	66	31	60
2.	QPR	42	24	11	7	67	33	59
3.	Man United	42	23	10	11	68	42	56
4.	Derby	42	21	11	10	75	58	53
5.	Leeds	42	21	9	12	65	46	51
6.	Ipswich	42	16	14	12	54	48	46
7.	Leicester	42	13	19	10	48	51	45
8.	Man City	42	16	12	15	64	46	43
9.	Tottenham	42	14	15	13	63	63	43
10.	Norwich	42	16	10	16	58	58	42
11.	Everton	42	15	12	15	60	66	42
12.	**Stoke**	**42**	**15**	**11**	**16**	**48**	**50**	**41**
13.	Middlesbrough	42	15	10	17	46	45	40
14.	Coventry	42	13	14	15	47	57	40
15.	Newcastle	42	15	9	18	71	62	39
16.	Aston Villa	42	11	17	14	51	59	39
17.	Arsenal	42	13	10	19	47	53	36
18.	West Ham	42	13	10	19	48	71	36
19.	Birmingham	42	13	7	22	57	75	33
20.	Wolverhampton	42	10	10	22	51	68	30
21.	Burnley	42	9	10	23	43	66	28
22.	Sheffield United	42	6	10	26	33	82	22

LEAGUE TABLES 1976-77

FIRST DIVISION	P	W	D	L	F	A	Pts
1. Liverpool	42	23	11	8	62	33	57
2. Man City	42	21	14	7	60	34	56
3. Ipswich	42	22	8	12	66	39	56
4. Aston Villa	42	22	7	13	76	50	51
5. Newcastle	42	18	13	11	64	49	49
6. Man United	42	18	11	13	71	62	47
7. WBA	42	16	13	13	62	56	45
8. Arsenal	42	16	11	15	64	59	43
9. Everton	42	14	14	14	62	64	42
10. Leeds	42	15	12	15	48	51	42
11. Leicester	42	12	18	12	47	60	42
12. Middlesbrough	42	14	13	15	40	45	41
13. Birmingham	42	13	12	17	63	61	38
14. QPR	42	13	12	17	47	52	38
15. Derby	42	9	19	14	50	55	37
16. Norwich	42	14	9	19	47	64	37
17. West Ham	42	11	14	17	46	65	36
18. Bristol City	42	11	13	18	38	48	35
19. Coventry	42	10	15	17	48	59	35
20. Sunderland	42	11	12	19	46	54	34
21. Stoke	**42**	**10**	**14**	**18**	**28**	**51**	**34**
22. Tottenham	42	12	9	21	48	72	33

LEAGUE TABLES 1977-78

SECOND DIVISION	P	W	D	L	F	A	Pts
1. Bolton	42	24	10	8	63	33	58
2. Southampton	42	22	13	7	70	39	57
3. Tottenham	42	20	16	6	83	49	56
4. Brighton	42	22	12	8	63	38	56
5. Blackburn	42	16	13	13	56	60	45
6. Sunderland	42	14	16	12	67	59	44
7. Stoke	**42**	**16**	**10**	**16**	**53**	**49**	**42**
8. Oldham	42	13	16	13	54	58	42
9. Crystal Palace	42	13	15	14	50	47	41
10. Fulham	42	14	13	15	49	49	41
11. Burnley	42	15	10	17	56	64	40
12. Sheffield United	42	16	8	18	62	73	40
13. Luton	42	14	10	18	54	52	38
14. Leyton Orient	42	10	18	14	43	49	38
15. Notts County	42	11	16	15	54	62	38
16. Millwall	42	12	14	16	49	57	38
17. Charlton Athletic	42	13	12	17	55	68	38
18. Bristol Rovers	42	13	12	17	61	77	38
19. Cardiff	42	13	12	17	51	71	38
20. Blackpool	42	12	13	17	59	60	37
21. Mansfield	42	10	11	21	49	69	31
22. Hull	42	8	12	22	34	52	28

LEAGUE TABLES 1978-79

SECOND DIVISION		P	W	D	L	F	A	Pts
1.	Brighton	42	23	10	9	72	39	56
2.	**Stoke**	**42**	**20**	**16**	**6**	**58**	**31**	**56**
3.	Sunderland	42	22	11	9	70	44	55
4.	Crystal Palace	42	19	19	4	51	24	55
5.	West Ham	42	18	15	10	69	37	49
6.	Notts County	42	14	16	12	48	60	44
7.	Fulham	42	13	15	14	49	45	42
8.	Preston NE	42	11	18	13	57	57	40
9.	Leyton Orient	42	15	10	17	51	51	40
10.	Burnley	42	14	12	16	51	57	40
11.	Newcastle	42	16	8	18	49	56	40
12.	Cambridge	42	12	16	14	44	52	40
13.	Cardiff	42	14	9	19	53	70	37
14.	Luton	42	13	10	19	60	55	36
15.	Leicester	42	10	16	16	41	50	36
16.	Bristol Rovers	42	13	10	19	47	58	36
17.	Wrexham	42	11	13	23	41	36	35
18.	Charlton Athletic	42	11	13	18	60	69	35
19.	Oldham	42	11	13	18	46	60	35
20.	Sheffield United	42	11	11	20	50	67	33
21.	Blackburn Rovers	42	9	10	23	39	71	28
22.	Millwall	42	9	9	24	36	52	27

Bill Bentley trains on the practice field. He was part of a Stoke City youth policy that Tony Waddington implemented.